Beaded Beauties
to crochet

Looking for a unique, yet refined, way to enhance your wardrobe? Elegantly graceful and distinctly personal crocheted jewelry is the ultimate accent for any outfit. You'll appreciate the exquisite detail of ten sophisticated necklaces and three bracelets, each made with slip stitches, colorful seed beads, and stylish focal beads. Re-create our samples, or express your personal sense of style by altering colors, beads, or length. Fashioning these tasteful trinkets isn't hard at all — more than a dozen photographs clearly illustrate the technique, which is easy to practice using pony beads and worsted weight yarn. So study our general instructions, and prepare to impress your friends with an array of beautiful beaded jewelry.

Designer: Susan Lutz Kenyon

A self-taught crocheter since 1969, Susan Lutz Kenyon began working with beads nearly 15 years ago. Inspired by her love of these two crafts, Susan began combining these art forms to create exquisite rope necklaces that showcase her collection of handmade beads. Susan enjoys teaching her innovative techniques in studio workshops, at conferences, and for a variety of guilds. In addition to being a Craft Yarn Council of America certified crochet teacher, Susan is a member of the Bead Society of Greater Chicago, where she served as Vice President/Program Chair for six years.

LEISURE ARTS, INC.
Little Rock, Arkansas

Please read General Instructions and Hints, pages 26–31, before beginning this project.

MATERIALS
Rope Beads
   Opaque E beads:
      White - 3 ounces (90 grams)
   Size 6/0 rochaille beads:
      Clear Gold - 1½ ounces (40 grams)
Cluster Beads
   Mini Glass Bead Mix:
      Silver and Gold - 1 package
      Dark Topaz - 1 package
      Gold - 1 package
Nylon cord, No. 2 - 1 spool White
Steel crochet hook, size 7 (1.65 mm)
Large eye beading needle
Darning needle
Hypo cement

ROPE
STRINGING PATTERN
String all the rope beads onto the nylon cord in the following order: 2 White, 1 Gold) repeated.

Leaving a long tail, ch 6; join with l st to form a ring.

Crochet 5 beads around using the Bead St until the rope is 34" (86.5 cm) long, ending by slip stitching the last 5 stitches without beads.

Finish off leaving a long tail.

FINISHING
JOINING ROPE ENDS
Secure the nylon cord tails in the rope.

CLUSTERS

- There are several ways of using beads to make Clusters. After you make your cluster, attach them and secure the beading thread in the rope (Diagram A, page 30).

- String one large bead, a medium bead, and a seed bead. Run the needle back through all the beads, skipping the seed bead.

- String a series of bugle beads with seed beads in between. Lay the string along the rope and sew down.

- String a series of bugle beads with seed beads in between; insert the needle where the thread is exiting the rope causing a loop to form.

- Randomly string beads from the packaged bead mixes.

- Let your creativity flow. Scoop up some beads on the needle and stretch them out or pull them snuggly together to form a loop. Sew the Clusters so that the necklace can be worn in any position. Do not sew any Clusters along back of necklace.

Hooked on Flowers

Please read General Instructions and Hints, pages 26–31, before beginning this project.

MATERIALS
Rope Beads
  Opaque E beads:
    Black - 8 ounces (230 grams)
  Size 6/0 Clear color-lined rochaille beads:
    Green, Pink, Blue, Orange, and
    Purple mix -1 package
Focal Beads
  Round glass beads
    Rainbow striped - 1 package of 6
    (2 small, 2 medium, and 2 large beads)
6 mm Star metal spacers - 6
Nylon cord, No. 2 - 1 spool Black
Steel crochet hook, size 7 (1.65 mm)
Large eye beading needle
Darning needle
Hypo cement

ROPE
The rope is worked in three sections: two Short Sections, each 4" (10 cm) long, and one Long Section, 23" (58.5 cm) long.

LONG SECTION
STRINGING PATTERN
String the rope beads onto the nylon cord in the following order:
32 Black, ♥ 1 Pink, 3 Black, 1 Green, 2 Pink, 1 Green, 3 Black, 1 Pink, 64 Black, 1 Blue, 3 Black, 1 Green, 2 Blue, 1 Green, 3 Black, 1 Blue, 64 1 Green, 3 Black, 1 Purple, 64 Black, 1 Blue, 3 Black, 1 Green, 2 Blue, 1 Green, 3 Black, 1 Blue, 64 Black, 1 Pink, 3 Black, 1 Green, 2 Pink, 1 Green, 3 Black, 1 Pink, 64 Black ♥, 1repeat from ♥ to ♥ once, 1 Purple, 3 Black, 1 Green, 2 Purple, 1 Green, 3 Black, 1 Purple, 32 Black.

Leaving a long tail, ch 6; join with sl st to form a ring.

Crochet 5 beads around using the Bead beads.

Finish off leaving a long tail.

FIRST SHORT SECTION
STRINGING PATTERN
String the rope beads onto the nylon cord in the following order:
32 Black, 1 Pink, 3 Black, 1 Green, 2 Pink, 1 Green, 3 Black, 1 Pink, 64 Black, 1 Purple, 3 Black, 1 Green, 2 Purple, 1 Green, 3 Black, 1 Purple, 64 Black, 1 Orange, 3 Black, 1 Green, 2 Orange, 1 Green, 3 Black, 1 Orange, 32 Black.

Work same as Long Section.

SECOND SHORT SECTION
STRINGING PATTERN
String the rope beads onto the nylon cord in the following order:
32 Black, 1 Blue, 3 Black, 1 Green, 2 Blue, 1 Green, 3 Black, 1 Blue, 64 Black, 1 Orange, 3 Black, 1 Green, 2 Orange, 1 Green, 3 Black, 1 Orange, 64 Black, 1 Purple, 3 Black, 1 Green, 2 Purple, 1 Green, 3 Black, 1 Purple, 32 Black.

Work same as Long Section.

FINISHING
Note: The Long Section will lie across the back of the neck.

To attach the Short Sections to the Long Section, follow Adding Focal Beads, page 29. String the beads onto the nylon cord tail from the Long Section in the following order:
  small focal bead
  star metal spacer
  clear rochaille bead (1 Pink on the first side or 1 Blue on the second side)
  star metal spacer
  medium focal bead
Run the nylon cord tail from Short Section through the beads strung on the Long Section nylon cord tail; secure the nylon cord tails in the rope.

Repeat for second side.

To connect the two Short Sections together, using nylon cord tail from the first Short Section, string the beads in the following order:

    large focal bead
    star metal spacer
    3 clear rochaille beads (1 Green, 1 Purple, 1 Green)
    star metal spacer
    large focal bead

Run the nylon cord tail from the second Short Section through the beads strung from the first Short Section; secure the nylon cord tails in the rope.

Hooked on Red

Please read General Instructions and Hints, pages 26–31, before beginning this project.

MATERIALS
Rope Beads
Opaque E beads:
Black - 3 ounces (85 grams)
Red - $^1/_2$ ounce (15 grams)
Focal Beads
Round glass beads:
Clear Red/Black striped - 1 package of 5
(2 small, 2 medium, and 1 large)
6 x 7 mm round metal spacers - 4
Nylon cord, No. 2 - 1 spool Black
Steel crochet hook, size 7 (1.65 mm)
Large eye beading needle
Darning needle
Hypo cement

ROPE
STRINGING PATTERN
String all the rope beads onto the nylon cord in the following order: 5 Black, (1 Red, 5 Black) repeated.

Leaving a long tail, ch 6; join with sl st to form a ring.

Crochet 5 beads around using the Bead St until the rope is 22" (56 cm) or the desired length, ending by slip stitching the last 5 stitches without a bead.

Finish off leaving a long tail.

FINISHING
String the focal beads onto one nylon cord tail in the following order:
small focal bead
metal spacer
medium focal bead
metal spacer
large focal bead
metal spacer
medium focal bead
metal spacer
small focal bead
Run the second nylon cord tail through the beads; secure the nylon cord tails in the rope.

Hooked on Squares

Please read General Instructions and Hints, pages 26–31, before beginning this project.

MATERIALS
Rope Beads
   Clear square glass beads:
      Purple-lined - 3 packages
      Green-lined - 3 packages

Focal Beads
   Clear square glass beads:
      Blue striped, Green-lined -
      1 package of 5
      (2 small, 2 medium, and 1 large)

5 mm Round metal spacers - 4
Nylon cord, No. 2 - 1 spool Dark Blue
Steel crochet hook, size 7 (1.65 mm)
Large eye beading needle
Darning needle
Hypo cement

ROPE
Randomly string all the rope beads onto the nylon cord.

Leaving a long tail, ch 6; join with sl st to form a ring.

Crochet 5 beads around using the Bead St until the rope is 26" (66 cm) long or the desired length, ending by slip stitching the last 5 stitches without beads.

Finish off leaving a long tail.

FINISHING
String the focal beads onto the nylon cord tail as follows:
   small focal bead
   metal spacer
   medium focal bead
   metal spacer
   large focal bead
   metal spacer
   medium focal bead
   metal spacer
   small focal bead
Run the second nylon cord tail through the beads strung on the first nylon cord tail; secure the nylon cord tails in the rope.

Hooked on Stripes

Please read General Instructions and Hints,
pages 26–31, before beginning this project.

MATERIALS

Rope Beads
  Opaque E beads:
    Black - 2$\frac{1}{2}$ ounces (70 grams)
    Striped - $\frac{1}{2}$ ounce (15 grams)
Focal Beads
  14 mm Roundel glass beads:
    Multi-colored - 4
  Round 10 mm Eye beads - 3

Nylon cord, No. 2 - 1 spool Black
Steel crochet hook, size 7 (1.65 mm)
Large eye beading needle
Darning needle, size 18
Hypo cement
Flexible coated craft wire
Tweezers
Wire Cutters

ROPE
STRINGING PATTERN

String all the rope beads onto the nylon cord in the following order: 7 Black, (1 Striped, 7 Black) repeated.

Leaving a long tail, ch 6; join with sl st to form a ring.

Crochet 5 beads around using the Bead St until the rope is 24" (61 cm) or the desired length, ending by slip stitching the last 5 stitches without beads.

Finish off leaving a long tail.

Thread darning needle with ending nylon cord tail and secure in same end of rope; repeat for beginning nylon cord tail.

FINISHING

The particular focal beads used have rough holes that will cut the nylon cord. In this case, we used flexible coated craft wire to string the focal beads *(see Adding Focal Beads, page 29)*.

Secure one end of the wire into the rope as before without knotting or gluing.

String the other end of the flexible coated craft wire through the focal beads in the following order: roundel bead, (eye bead, roundel bead) 3 times.

Secure second end of wire in same manner as first end of wire; do not cut wire. Run wire back through the focal beads and secure second wire end in rope as before. Using tweezers, run this end inside a nearby rope bead.

Hooked on White

Please read General Instructions and Hints, pages 26–31, before beginning this project.

MATERIALS

Rope Beads
Opaque White E beads:
2½ ounces (70 grams)
Focal Beads
Assorted shapes Clear/White glass beads:
1 package
Assorted shapes foil-lined glass beads:
1 package

Bead caps - 4
Nylon cord, No. 2 - 1 spool White
Steel crochet hook, size 7 (1.65 mm)
Darning needle
Large eye beading needle
Hypo cement

ROPE

String all the rope beads onto the nylon cord.

Leaving a long tail, ch 6; join with sl st to form a ring.

Crochet 5 beads around using the Bead St until the rope is approximately 19½" (49.5 cm) long, ending by slip stitching the last 5 stitches without beads.

Finish off leaving a long tail.

FINISHING

Each side will have two bead caps, one with the cup facing the rope and the second facing the focal beads. Both strands will go in the same bead cap, one on each side.
Long Strand: You can string the focal beads in any order for 9½" (24 cm).
Short Strand: You can string the focal beads in any order for 7" (18 cm).

We placed rope beads right after the bead caps and throughout the strands. Have fun stringing your strands!
String the Long Strand with the nylon cord tail from one end of the rope and the Short Strand with the nylon cord tail from the other end of the rope.
Secure the nylon cord tails in the rope.

MATERIALS
Rope Beads
    Opaque Black E beads:
        $2^3/_4$ ounces (80 grams)
    Size 6/0 beads:
        Brown - 2 ounces (60 grams)
        Gold - 2 ounces (60 grams)
Focal Bead
    $1^1/_8$" (2.75 cm) diameter metal shank button
Nylon cord, No. 2 - 1 spool Brown
Steel crochet hook, size 7 (1.65 mm)
Darning needle, size 18
Large eye beading needle
Hypo cement

Please read General Instructions and Hints, pages 26–31, before beginning this project.

ROPE

Randomly string all the rope beads onto the nylon cord.

Leaving a long tail, ch 6; join with sl st to form a ring.

Crochet 5 beads around using the Bead St until the rope is 23" (58.5 cm) or the desired length to fit comfortable over the head, ending by slip stitching the last 5 stitches without beads.

Finish off leaving a long tail.

Thread darning needle with one nylon cord tail and secure button to rope end; secure nylon cord tail in same side of rope.
Thread darning needle with second nylon cord tail and secure button to rope end; secure nylon cord tails in same end of rope.

This closure can be worn in the front or the back.

MATERIALS

Rope Beads
   Opaque White E beads:
      $3^3/_4$ ounces (105 grams)
   Size 6/0 Clear, silver-lined rochaille beads:
      $3^3/_4$ ounces (105 grams)
   Iridescent Green E beads:
      $1^3/_4$ ounces (50 grams)

Dangle Beads
   Assorted shaped Pink glass beads -
      1 package
   Wire covered glass beads - 4
1 cm Swirl bead caps - 2

10 mm double ring - 2
7 mm jump rings
Nylon cord, No. 2 - 1 spool White
Steel crochet hook, size 7 (1.65 mm)
2" (5 cm) long eye pins
$1^1/_2$" (4 cm) long eye pins
2" (5 cm) long head pins (flat head)
$1^1/_2$" (4 cm) long head pins (flat head)
Darning needle
Large eye beading needle
Hypo cement
Needle nose pliers

Hooked on a Lariat

Please read General Instructions and Hints, pages 26–31 before beginning this project.

ROPE
STRINGING PATTERN

String all the rope beads onto the nylon cord in the following order: (White, Clear, Green) repeated.

Leaving a long tail, ch 6; join with sl st to form a ring.

Crochet 5 beads around using Bead St until the rope is 44" (112 cm) long or the desired length, ending by slip stitching the last 5 stitches without beads.

Finish off leaving a long tail.

FINISHING

For a Lariat, the rope ends are not connected.

FIRST END

String swirl bead cap onto nylon cord tail with design facing away from rope. Loop the nylon cord tail two or three times around a 10 mm double ring. Adjust the nylon cord so that the ring is snug against the cap and the cap is snug against the rope. Secure nylon cord tail in the rope.
To make Dangles, string beads as desired onto eye pins and head pins. To make long dangles, connect headpins to eyes on eye pins. Make 3 dangles for each end of rope. Use 7 mm jump rings to attach dangles to the 10 mm double ring.

Repeat for second end.

This necklace can be worn with both ends hanging down or looped into a loose knot.

Hooked on the Primaries

Please read General Instructions and Hints, pages 26–31, before beginning this project.

MATERIALS

Size 6/0 Clear seed beads:
2³/₄ ounces (80 grams)
Nylon cord, No. 2 -
1 spool Primary Variegated
Steel crochet hook, size 7
(1.65 mm)
Darning needle
Large eye beading needle
Hypo cement
Clear nail polish

ROPE

String all the beads onto the nylon cord except 8 beads to be used on the Tassel.

Leaving a long tail, ch 6; join with sl st to form a ring.

Crochet 5 beads around using the Bead St until the rope is approximately 30¹/₂" (77.5 cm) long, ending by slip stitching the last 5 stitches without beads.

Finish off leaving a long tail.

FINISHING

Secure the ending nylon cord tail 5¹/₄" (13 cm) up from beginning end of the rope.

TASSEL

From the nylon cord spool, cut two strands each of Yellow, Red, Blue, and Green.
Holding the strands together, fold in half and tie a knot at the fold, slipping a crochet hook in the loop. Tighten the knot. Carefully slip the hook out of the loop.
Thread the darning needle with the beginning nylon cord tail and sew the Tassel to the rope several times to secure the Tassel; then secure the tail in the rope.
Thread a bead onto each nylon cord tail on the Tassel, knotting each strand securely about 2" down from Tassel knot. Clip each end close to the knot, cover knot with a drop of clear nail polish to hold knot.

Hooked on Black and White

Please read General Instructions and Hints, pages 26–31, before beginning this project.

MATERIALS

Rope Beads
  Opaque E beads:
    Black - 1¼ ounces (35 grams)
    White - 1¼ ounces (35 grams)
  Rochaille E beads, Clear silver-lined:
    1¼ ounces (35 grams)

Focal Bead
  1³/₄" (4.5 cm) Cross Pendant
  1 cm Swirl bead caps - 2
  Nylon cord, No. 2 - 1 spool White
  Steel crochet hook, size 7 (1.65 mm)
  Darning needle
  Large eye beading needle
  Hypo cement

ROPE
STRINGING PATTERN
String all the rope beads (except for 6 Opaque White beads used with focal bead cross pendant) onto the nylon cord in the following order: Black, White, Black, (Clear, Black, White, Black) repeated.

Leaving a long tail, ch 6; join with sl st to form a ring.

Crochet 5 beads around using the Bead St until the rope is 34" (86.5 cm) long or the desired length, ending by slip stitching the last 5 stitches without beads.

Finish off leaving a long tail.

FINISHING
String the focal beads onto nylon cord
tail in the following order:
    Swirl bead cap (to cup rope end)
    3 White rope beads
    cross pendant
    3 White rope beads
    swirl bead cap (to cup rope end)
[Rope beads fit under the Cross pendant.]
Run the second nylon cord tail through
the caps and beads strung on the first
nylon cord tail; secure the nylon cord tails
in the rope.

Bracelets

Please read General Instructions and Hints, pages 26–31, before beginning these projects.

Hooked on Confetti

MATERIALS
Size 6/0 Multi-colored rochaille beads:
    ³/4 ounce (20 grams)
Nylon cord, No. 2 - 1 spool White
Steel crochet hook, size 7 (1.65 mm)
Darning needle
Large eye beading needle
Hypo cement

ROPE
Randomly string all the beads onto the nylon cord.

Leaving a long tail, ch 6; join with sl st to form a ring.

Crochet 5 beads around using the Bead St until the rope is 8" (20.5 cm) long or the desired length to fit snuggle over the hand at the knuckles, ending by slip stitching the last 5 stitches without beads.

Finish off leaving a long tail.

FINISHING
Secure the nylon cord tails in the rope,

MATERIALS
Size 6/0 Clear seed beads:
  $^3/_4$ ounce (20 grams)
Nylon cord, No. 2 - 1 spool
  Blue Variegated
Steel crochet hook, size 7
  (1.65 mm)
"S" swirl dangles - 7
Swirl bead caps - 2
Toggle Clasp set
7 mm jump rings - 7
Darning needle
Large eye beading needle
Hypo cement
Needle nose pliers

ROPE
String all the beads onto the nylon cord.

Leaving a long tail, ch 6; join with sl st to form a ring.

Crochet 5 beads around using the Bead St until the rope is 8" (20.5 cm) or the desired length, ending by slip stitching the last 5 stitches without beads.

Finish off leaving a long tail.

FINISHING
Thread the darning needle with the beginning nylon cord tail. String 1 bead cap (to cup rope). Loop the nylon cord twice through the circle part of the clasp and run back through the bead cap. Secure the nylon cord tail in the rope.

Thread the darning needle with the ending nylon cord tail. String bead cap (to cup rope), 3 rope beads and the bar part of the toggle clasp. Loop the nylon cord again through the toggle bar. Run the nylon cord back through the rope beads and the bead cap. Secure the nylon cord tail in the rope.

Use the pliers to open each of the jump rings by twisting one half lightly to the side, looping each through a rope bead evenly around; attach a swirl charm and close each jump ring.

Please read General Instructions and Hints, pages 26–31, before beginning this project.

MATERIALS

Rope Beads
    Opaque E beads:
        Black - 1 ounce (30 grams)
        Red - approx. 100-150
Focal Beads
    Size 10/0 seed beads:
        Turquoise - approx. 100-150
    Oval Ladhaki bead - 1

Nylon cord, No. 2 - 1 spool Black
Beading thread
Steel crochet hook, size 7 (1.65 mm)
Darning needle, size 18
Large eye beading needle
Hypo cement

ROPE
STRINGING PATTERN

String the rope beads onto the nylon cord in the following order: 5 Black, (1 Red, 5 Black) repeated.

Leaving a long tail, ch 6; join with sl st to form a ring.

Crochet 5 beads around using the Bead St until the rope is 8" (20.5 cm) long or long enough to fit snuggly over the knuckle part of the hand, ending by slip stitching the last 5 stitches without beads.

Finish off leaving a long tail.

FINISHING
LOOPED STRAND

Thread the beading needle with a 36" (91.5 cm) length of beading thread. Double the thread and knot the ends together.
Insert the needle in one end of the rope and come out next to the first Red rope bead. String enough turquoise beads onto the beading needle to reach half way to the next Red rope bead. Lay the turquoise beads on the rope. Insert the needle from bottom to top through the Black rope bead to the left of the turquoise beads. Insert the needle from top to bottom through the last two turquoise beads (backstitch made).

Pull beading thread tight. String enough turquoise beads needed to reach the next Red rope bead. Insert the needle from bottom to top straight into the Red rope bead; do not backstitch. Continue in same manner until you reach the end of the rope. Secure the beading thread in the rope.

LARGE FOCAL BEAD

Using nylon cord tails, add the focal bead (see Adding Focal Beads, page 29).

Each necklace and bracelet in this leaflet are composed of a crocheted, beaded "rope", and will be referred to as a rope in the individual instructions.

CROCHET HINTS

- Drink lots of water while working. Besides being good for you, it will make you get up and move around every once in a while. When you get up, rotate your shoulders and neck, and flex your hands.

- Sit in a comfortable chair to do your crocheting. Do not work with your elbows on a table; that is hard on your elbows and back.

- When working with Black cord and Black beads, lay a White cloth in your lap. It will help you to better see the work.

- Keep a needle handy. To correct a mistake, some of the crocheting may need to be taken out (unraveled). A tapestry needle will help pull out the loop that needs to go back onto the hook.

ABBREVIATIONS

ch	chain
sl st	slip stitch
YO	yarn over

GAUGE / TENSION

The work should not be real tight but it should not be real loose. Generally, the beaded rope should have very little nylon cord showing and be fairly firm. Use a larger hook if the work is too tight or if the hook is piercing the nylon cord; use a smaller hook if it is too loose.

MATERIALS
ROPE BEADS

Size 6/O seed/rochaille beads and E beads have been used for the projects in this leaflet. It takes approximately 3½ ounces (100 grams) of beads to make a 26" (66 cm) length of rope, and 4¾ ounces (135 grams) for a 32" (81.5 cm) necklace. For a 7" (18 cm) long bracelet, it takes approximately 43" (109 cm) of beads.

FOCAL BEADS

Focal beads are beads that create a center of interest after the crocheted rope is completed, and are usually added using the nylon cord tails.

TWISTED NYLON CORD

Omega nylon cord, No. 2, was used to make these projects. Twisted nylon cord is preferred when working with size 6/0 seed/rochaille or E beads. Nylon cord doesn't fray during the crochet process.

Choose a nylon cord color that matches the majority of beads used or will show through the clear beads. Nylon cord is the least expensive part of your creation, so don't skimp on quality.

STEEL CROCHET HOOK

A steel crochet hook, size 7 that is 1.65 mm was used for the projects in this leaflet. Keep in mind that steel crochet hooks vary by manufacturer, so check your hook.

LARGE EYE BEADING NEEDLE is used to string the beads onto the nylon cord. It looks like a piece of wire. It is split open but secured at both ends. Open the "eye" and loop the cord through.

DARNING NEEDLE, is used for hiding the nylon cord tails in the rope. These needles have large eyes and sharp points.

BEADING THREAD, such as Nymo, is used to make a harness. The harness allows you to string beads onto nylon cord if a large eye beading needle is not available

HYPO CEMENT that comes in a tube for fine detail work, is used for securing nylon cord knots in the rope. It is usually found in the bead department.

OTHER USEFUL ITEMS
Needle nose pliers
Tweezers
Clear nail polish
Thimble
Flexible coated craft wire

STRINGING BEADS

Stringing the bead pattern onto the nylon cord can take longer than the actual crocheting of the rope, but the beautiful patterns that emerge are well worth the effort.

Hint: To keep the nylon cord end from unraveling, dip the end in clear nail polish and drape it over the center of the spool to dry before threading it onto the large eye needle.

To string the beads, slip a long piece of the nylon cord, still attached to the spool, through the large eye beading needle.

Using the large eye beading needle, scoop up the beads and slide them down the needle and onto the nylon cord. Continue stringing beads, as specified in individual instructions, until you have strung all your beads, unless otherwise specified.

Always leave a few beads on the nylon cord where it is doubled so that the nylon cord does not slip out of the eye.

Hint: When pulling the beads onto the nylon cord, hold the needle by the eye. This puts less stress on the eye and will not be as likely to break.

Hint: Do not use any beads that do not slide easily down over the eye of the needle.

HARNESS

When large eye beading needles are not available, a beading needle can be used. Since the nylon cord will not fit into the eye of a beading needle, a harness is used.

Note: We have used a tapestry needle, bedspread weight cotton, and worsted weight yarn for clarity.

To make a Harness, insert a 4" (10 cm) piece of beading thread through the eye of the needle. Tie a square knot in the thread (left over right and right over left). Holding both loose ends of the thread, pull the circle open until the knot is secured. Loop the nylon cord through the harness and proceed to string beads *(Fig. 1).*

Fig. 1

needle

harness

nylon cord

Hint: When stringing beads with small holes, be sure the knot in the harness is at the side of the harness and not directly behind the eye of the needle nor where the nylon cord is looped over.

Note: We have used worsted weight yarn and pony beads for clarity. You may want to practice the Bead Stitch in the larger scale before beginning your project.

BEAD STITCH
(abbreviated Bead St)

Definition: A sl st worked with a bead.

Insert hook in next ch *(Fig. 2a)*. Slide a bead down the nylon cord and close to the work *(Fig. 2b)*, YO *(Fig. 2c)*, and draw through st and loop on the hook *(Fig. 2d)*.

Fig. 2a

Fig. 2b

Fig. 2c

Fig. 2d

THE ROPE

> Hint: Before beginning to crochet, double check the stringing pattern.

Crocheting the rope is fairly simple but takes practice. If you lengthen or shorten the ropes, you will need to adjust the number of beads accordingly.

Leave an 18" (45.5 cm) nylon cord tail so that there is enough to run through focal beads and knot into the rope to finish.

Foundation round:
Chain 6 and join with a sl st to form a ring.
Insert the hook into the next ch [under top loop and back ridge (Fig. 3a)]. Slide a bead down the nylon cord close to the work, YO and draw through both loops on the hook (Figs. 2b–d, page 27): one Bead St made.

Fig. 3a

Repeat this until there are 5 Bead Sts (Fig. 3b). At this point you should be around to the first Bead St.

Fig. 3b

When crocheting the rope, you do not "chain up" to get to the next round, but work in a continuous round, causing the beads to spiral on the rope.

From now on, you will work Bead Sts into the Bead Sts.
Insert the hook in the hole of the first Bead St **after** the Bead (Fig. 4a). Slip the bead in this stitch far enough to the back of the hook so that it is locked under the nylon cord, then slide the next bead down from the nylon cord close to the work, YO (Fig. 4b), and draw the nylon cord through the stitch and the loop on the rope.
This locks the previous bead to the outside of the work.
Continue working Bead Sts until the specific rope length has been crocheted.

Fig. 4a

Fig. 4b

After you have worked several rounds, notice that beads in previous rounds sit with the holes running vertically to the rope, while the beads on the last rnd worked of the rope sit with the holes running horizontal (Fig. 5a). If a bead in the rope doesn't have the holes sitting vertically, it means the bead was not locked to the outside correctly or it was skipped. Unravel the nylon cord and correct it.

Fig. 5a

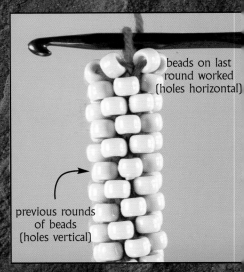

beads on last round worked (holes horizontal)

previous rounds of beads (holes vertical)

Every once in a while, look down at the top of the rope; there should be 5 beads standing with the holes horizontal to the work *(Fig. 5b)*.

Fig. 5b

Before finishing the rope as a necklace or bracelet without a closure, be sure the rope is long enough to slip over your head or hand before finishing the crocheting.

To finish the crocheting, work one final round in the same way as the previous rounds but do not add a bead with the stitch (sl st in each sl st around). This allows the beads on the last round to sit vertically as the other beads in the rope *(Fig. 6)*.
Finish off leaving an 18" (45.5 cm) nylon cord tail and cut it from the spool.

Fig. 6

FINISHING
ADDING FOCAL BEADS

For a rope with Focal bead(s) and no closure, thread the darning needle with one nylon cord tail and string the focal bead(s). It may be necessary to use the beading needle and harness if you are using small-holed focal beads and spacers.

After you have strung all of the elements, re-thread the darning needle and insert it into the other end of the rope in the opposite position from the where the second nylon cord tail lays, and through center of the rope with the needle coming out about a $1/2$" to 1" (1.25 to 2.5 cm) from the end of the rope, being careful not to pierce a bead.

Pull the needle through the work. Pliers or a thimble may be useful here.

Repeat for second nylon cord tail, threading the nylon cord tail through the focal beads and into the opposite rope end *(Fig. 7a)*.

Fig. 7a

Grabbing each nylon cord tail on each side of the focal bead(s), pull very tight simultaneously to line up the rope ends. Hold the focal bead(s) and the rope so that they stay firmly together. Starting on one side, insert the darning needle under a stitch in the rope, and pull the needle through the loop to form a knot *(Fig. 7b)*, keeping the tension tight in the focal bead area.

Fig. 7b

As the knot is pulled closed, push it down in between the beads. Put a drop of hypo cement on the knot made and pull the nylon cord tight. The knot will be pulled into the rope as you travel to the next area.

Repeat this sequence, slanting the darning needle through the rope (Diagram A).

Diagram A

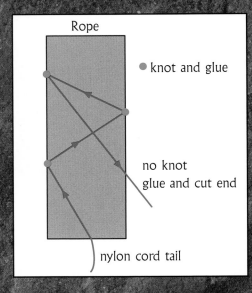

After making the last knot, insert the needle through the rope, but have it slanting down as it goes through the rope. Do not form a knot.

Put a drop of hypo cement in the hole where the nylon cord exits the rope. Lay a sharp pair of scissors parallel to the work and around the nylon cord. Pull hard on the nylon cord and snip it. The nylon cord tail will disappear into the work.

Secure the second nylon cord tail in the same manner.

Wire may be used when stringing Focal beads if the bead holes are rough and may cut the nylon cord. Use flexible coated craft wire that is the color of the nylon cord used in crocheting the rope.

Cut a long piece of wire 5 times the length of the beads to be strung. Thread it through the eye of a darning needle. Bend the short end of the wire so it lies next to the main piece of wire. Run this wire through the rope. However, instead of knotting it, weave the wire back and forth several times through the rope. Work it one last time, slanting the needle down. Bring it out the other side and cut the end, leaving a short piece. With tweezers, insert this end inside one of the beads. With this end secured, thread beads onto wire and secure second wire end.

For a rope with Focal bead(s) and closure, you will crochet two ropes of the same length. You will add the focal bead(s) in same manner as rope with focal bead(s) and no closure. Then add the closure to the other ends in same manner as Hooked On Dangles Bracelet, page 23.

CLOSING A ROPE

For a rope with no Focal bead and no closure, hold the two ends of the rope together. Using one nylon cord tail, go through one bead on the same side, through a bead on the opposite side and down through the next bead over, and over and through a bead on the first side (*Fig. 8*). Continue around and pull tight. Secure nylon cord tails within rope (*Diagram A*).

Fig. 8

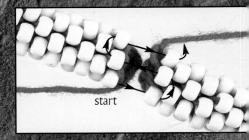

Secure the second nylon cord tail in same manner.

CORRECTING BEADS

As you are crocheting the rope, there may be a bead that was strung in the wrong order or a bead that is an odd shape that needs to be removed. You remove glass beads by breaking them. There are two ways to break the glass bead:

First, place a needle through the bead hole on top of the nylon cord to act as a buffer between the bead and the nylon cord. Using pliers and a cloth to cover the bead (to prevent the bead from flying out), place the jaws of the pliers over the hole of the bead and squeeze hard (*Fig. 9a*).

Fig. 9a

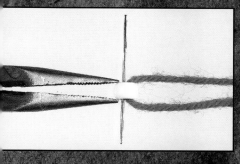

Second, if the bead is too strong to be broken this way, place the jaws over the sides of the bead *(Fig. 9b). (Note: This way increases the chances of cutting the nylon cord!)*

Fig. 9b

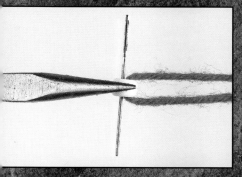

When continuing to crochet after a bead has been removed, it is necessary to make a space in the rope where the correct bead will be placed. When the space is reached, sl st without a bead. Mark this space with a piece of contrasting nylon cord until a correct bead can be inserted. Continue with the Bead St to complete the rope.

To fill the space with the new bead, cut a long piece of nylon cord and thread it onto the darning needle. About 1" (2.5 cm) away from the space, insert the needle into the rope and pull it through, leaving a long tail, 5" to 6" (12.5 cm to 15 cm). Make a knot as before between the beads and come up into the space for the new bead.

Remove the needle and thread the correct bead onto the nylon cord and slide it into position in the rope space. Insert the re-threaded darning needle back into the space and have it come out the other side of the rope. Complete the knotting sequence as before *(Diagram A, page 30).* Secure the beginning nylon cord tail to the rope as before.

ADDING NEW CORD

Adding a new nylon cord may be necessary if not enough beads were strung before beginning or if the nylon cord breaks.
If not enough beads were strung, leave a long tail with one bead left on the end before cutting the nylon cord from the spool. String more beads, in stringing pattern, if applicable, onto the nylon cord still attached to the spool. The new beads will be on the new end of the nylon cord. Hold the old and the new ends together. Make one Bead St using both the old end with one bead on it and the new end. Drop the old end and continue with the new end. After crocheting a couple inches, go back and secure both tails as in Adding Focal Beads, page 29.
If the nylon cord breaks, unravel some of the crocheting so that there is a long tail. Remove all the beads except one and complete as above.

BEAD HINTS

- If the focal bead doesn't have a hole large enough to hide the rope ends, other beads with large holes, such a donuts, can be used. Beads with a concaved end area fit around the rope especially well, as do bead caps.

- When using more than one focal bead, it is best to have an odd number of beads. This allows the work to curve, look symmetrical, and the nylon cord is less likely to show.

- To keep a bead with a large hole from moving too much and to keep it in line, go through the bead at least twice with each nylon cord tail.

- When doing the downward slants, continue until the darning needle eventually comes out of the end of the rope again. Go through the focal bead and up into the opposite side of the rope a second time with each nylon cord tail. You have now gone through the focal bead four times. Secure the nylon cord tails as previously instructed.

- When stringing one color of beads or random mixes, put the beads in a shallow dish. Use the needle to scoop up the beads.

- Packages of pre-mixed colors of beads are available in stores. To make a custom mixture, buy two or more different colors. Stir them together in a dish before stringing. Be sure to mix more than is needed as it is almost impossible to make the exact mix a second time.

Materials Information

For your convenience, the specific beads used to create the photography models are listed below.

HOOKED ON CREATIVITY
Westrim Opaque E beads
   Style #4996-ZE-008 White
Westrim Silver line rochaille
   Beads - Clear Gold
Blue Moon Mini Glass Bead mix
   #51375 Silver and gold
   #51285 Dark Topaz
   #51275 Lt Topaz (Gold)
Omega Cord, No. 2 - #01 White

HOOKED ON FLOWERS
Westrim Opaque E beads
   Style #4996-ZE-002 Black
Westrim 6/0 Color lined rochaille beads
   #4998 mix
Blue Moon beads
   #53205 Round rainbow striped glass beads
   #52895 Metal star beads
Omega Cord, No. 2 - #20 Black

HOOKED ON RED
Westrim Opaque E beads
   Style #4996-ZE-002 Black
   Style #4996-ZE-008 Red
Blue Moon round glass beads
   Red/Black striped
Blue Moon 6 x 7 mm round metal beads
   #54885 or #54915
Omega Cord, No. 2 - #20 Black

HOOKED ON SQUARES
Blue Moon square glass beads
   #58675 Blue, Purple-lined
   #58635 Blue, Green-lined
Blue Moon Art Glass
   #58655 Blue and Green striped
   #BB3696-02 Gold
Omega Cord, No. 2 - #22 Royal

HOOKED ON STRIPES
Westrim Opaque E beads
   Style #4996-ZE-002 Black
Westrim bead glass striped 5/0 beads
   Style #4985 Large Striped opaque
Westrim eye beads
   Style #23542 Glass Assorted size
Blue Moon 14 mm roundel beads
   #55205 Multi-colored
Omega Cord, No. 2 - #20 Black

HOOKED ON WHITE
Westrim Opaque E beads
   Style #4996-ZE-00X White
Westrim glass beads of assorted shapes
Westrim foil-lined assorted shapes
Omega Cord, No. 2 - #01 White

HOOKED ON A BUTTON
Westrim size 6/0 beads
   Black, silver lined
   Brown, silver lined
Omega Cord, No. 2 - #47 Grape

THE SCIENCE OF

HENSIVE SCHOOL
Books)
ack on

JUNGLE
MEDICINE

by
JEREMY SMITH
Consultant
SHAHINA GHAZANFAR

355083

Quiz no: 209107
BL: 8.5
Points: 1.0
IL: MY

CONTENTS

When we get ill, we sometimes visit the pharmacist or doctor who gives us medicine containing **drugs** to treat the sickness. Around a quarter of all drugs we use today contain plant chemicals, and about half of these were originally found in the rich **habitat** of the **rainforests**. Today, scientists continue to investigate jungle plants in the hope of finding a new drug that may fight diseases such as **cancer**, for example.

A RICH RESOURCE

All plants produce chemicals called **phytochemicals** (phyto is a Greek word for plant). Some types of phytochemicals have healing properties that can help people fight diseases. Scientists search for new phytochemicals in plants from all over the world; they also look for useful chemicals in our herbs, fruits and vegetables such as garlic, berries and broccoli. Scientists searching for new phytochemicals concentrate their efforts in the rainforests because they provide the richest source of plant **species** in the world. The numbers are so great that less than one percent of the rainforest's millions of species have been studied by scientists so far.

A WORLD OF RESEARCH

Today, over 100 **pharmaceutical** companies are carrying out research on rainforest plants for possible drugs and cures for diseases ranging from simple infections to cancer and AIDS. Most work to develop new drugs is done by teams of scientists who work at universities and at drug companies. Many different people are needed to make up a research team. **Botanists** carry out the plant research and collect the plants from the wild, while **ethnobotanists** talk to rainforest people to discover valuable information on medicinal plants. Environmentalists may help to make sure that the

Finding useful plants in the rainforest is a difficult job. While some may be potential life savers, others may contain deadly poisons.

An Indian shaman holds medicinal plants gathered from the forest village of Aska aja, Venezuela.

A research scientist extracts potentially valuable compounds from plant matter.

environment is not damaged by the plant collections. Back at the laboratory, chemists extract many chemicals from the plant material. Biochemists and **cell biologists** test the chemicals to find out what effects they may have on living cells. **Toxicologists** and **geneticists** check to see whether there are any dangers in using the drugs, and what the best dose would be.

A RACE AGAINST TIME?

The search for medicinal plants in tropical forests faces one great threat: these rainforests are being destroyed at an alarming rate. Because of **deforestation** not only are the plants lost, but the people who live there have to leave their home and environment, and their great knowledge of medicinal plants is dispersed, and eventually lost and forgotten forever.

Plants have been used for medicines all over the world for thousands of years. Some of the traditional uses of plants may have no real medicinal value, but others certainly did. Some have been found to contain powerful **drugs** on which a lot of our modern medicines are based. The scientific search for drugs from plants started during the 19th century.

An open page from Das Buch der Nature, written in 1475. It is thought to be the oldest published book on plant medicine in the world.

A LONG HISTORY

Plants have probably been used as medicine for as long as man has existed. Written records tell us that Greeks and people from the Middle East used medicinal plants around the 5th Century BC, while around 2,700 BC the Chinese emperor and **herbalist** Shen Nung compiled a book of plant medicine called the *Pen Tsao Kang Mu*. In ancient Egypt, medicinal plants have been recovered from Giza pyramids by archaeologists. By the 1st century AD, knowledge on medicinal plants was considerable. In 78 AD, the Greek physician Dioscorides wrote *De Materia Medica*, a book which listed over 600 medicinal plants and influenced physcians for hundreds of years. The blending of science with **botany** began in 16th-century Switzerland, where a doctor called Paracelsus started to explore ways of using of plant chemicals to cure the sick. In 18th-century England, a doctor and botanist called William

SCIENCE CONCEPTS

CHINESE MEDICINE

Chinese medicine has traditionally been very different from that used in western countries. It looks at health holistically, and uses herbs, diet, massage, relaxation and exercise to combat sickness. Healing plants are mentioned in Chinese writings dating back to 2,700 BC, and today thousands of plant substances are used to cure sickness. Remedies such as ginseng and Ginkgo biloba are still used today to treat a range of illnesses from coughs to asthma.

A medicine man from Indonesia gathers rainforest plants he will use for healing.

Withering studied the use of plants as medicine, and discovered that the foxglove (*digitalis*) could treat heart problems.

THE BIRTH OF PHYTOCHEMISTRY

In 1803 the German pharmacist Friedrich Sertürner became the first person to isolate powerful chemicals called **alkaloids** from plants. The science of **phytochemistry** (the study of the chemicals in plants) and the search for medicinal plants had begun. Botany became popular and was taught at the famous universities of the time. Treatments for diseases that had plagued mankind for many years were discovered, including a cure for **malaria** called quinine, made from the bark of the cinchona tree; and aspirin, from the bark of willow. Once the active ingredients were known, plant scientists were able to copy the chemicals in the safety of the laboratory.

CHANGING FORTUNES

By the 1950s, scientists had discovered a number of important drugs from tropical forest plants. Scientists were also increasingly able to make new drugs by mixing up combinations of existing chemicals. By the late 1970s, however, the spectacular successes in producing drugs from the rainforests had begun to dry up. Little money was spent on searching plants for potential cures, and several organizations abandoned their plant research programmes. Then in the 1980s, with advanced methods of analyzing and researching plants, scientists turned back to nature. This led to many new discoveries, including one of the most potent anti-**cancer** medications in use today (*see page 28-29*).

The leaves of the healing herb foxglove are today powdered into a drug that keeps millions of heart patients alive.

SCIENCE SNAPSHOT

In a recent report, the World Health Organization (WHO) estimated that 80% of the population of developing countries still relies mainly on plant drugs to treat their sick. This is mostly because these treatments are easily available and cheap to buy, but also because they do not carry the side-effects many prescription drugs have.

Botanists and **ethnobotanists** are experts in finding plants, as they know exactly the types of places, or **habitats**, that different plants live in. They can identify plants that have already been studied and named, and can look at the features of new, undiscovered plants and decide how they should be classified. Botanists also have expert knowledge about the structure and **chemistry** of plants and how they work.

These botanists are identifying and cataloguing plant specimens in Guyana.

TRACKING DOWN PLANTS

Searching for medicinal plants in the **rainforest** may seem like a good idea due to the number of **species** present, but this also creates the problem of where to start looking. Scientists estimate that only 1% of the world's 3-4 million known species of plants have so far been examined for their medicinal properties. The first **sampling** technique involves collection of as many different species as possible to be tested, but avoiding those plants that have already been tested in the laboratory. A study plot the size of a couple of football fields is marked off, and researchers examine every plant within that area. Using this approach, the National **Cancer** Institute took over 45,000 plant samples and discovered **drugs** including taxol (*see page 28-29*). A second technique involves looking for plants with chemicals that make them naturally resistant to specific pests and diseases as these chemicals may have similar effects in humans. For example, a plant with natural pest-fighting defenses might contain chemicals that will provide humans with the same defence against diseases such as **malaria**. Finally, botanists can

SCIENCE CONCEPTS

NAMING PLANTS

Carl Linnaeus was an eighteenth century Swedish botanist who developed a system for naming and classifying plants. Each plant was given a two-word name: the first word was the genus (or group) name and the second was its own specific name. Writing the names in Latin meant they could be used and understood by scientists all over the world. These names are still used today: for example, the name for a daisy is Bellis perennis, and ivy is Hedera helix. The plant on the right is a sample of Triumfetta bartramia, collected and named by Linnaeus.

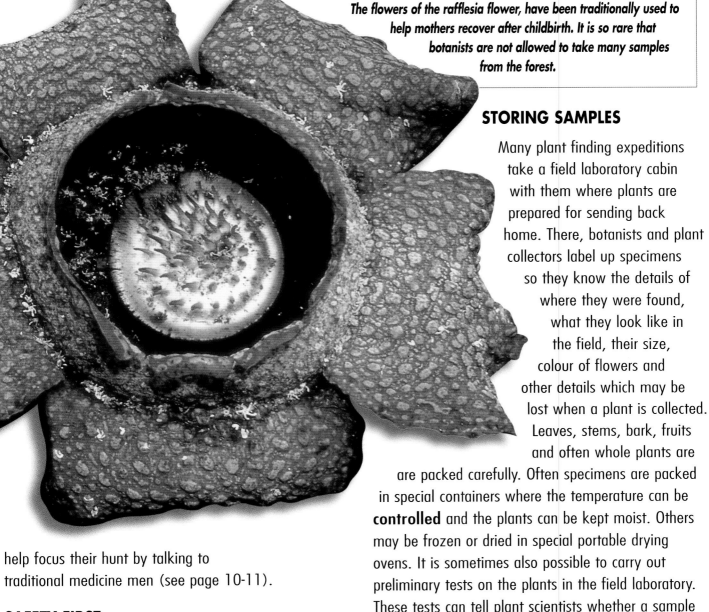

The flowers of the rafflesia flower, have been traditionally used to help mothers recover after childbirth. It is so rare that botanists are not allowed to take many samples from the forest.

STORING SAMPLES

Many plant finding expeditions take a field laboratory cabin with them where plants are prepared for sending back home. There, botanists and plant collectors label up specimens so they know the details of where they were found, what they look like in the field, their size, colour of flowers and other details which may be lost when a plant is collected. Leaves, stems, bark, fruits and often whole plants are are packed carefully. Often specimens are packed in special containers where the temperature can be **controlled** and the plants can be kept moist. Others may be frozen or dried in special portable drying ovens. It is sometimes also possible to carry out preliminary tests on the plants in the field laboratory. These tests can tell plant scientists whether a sample might contain useful chemicals or not.

help focus their hunt by talking to traditional medicine men (see page 10-11).

SAFETY FIRST

Whether they know exactly what they are looking for or not, botanists have to take a lot of care when they are plant-hunting. **Rainforests** and other remote places can be dangerous, so the scientists must follow safety precautions at all times in order to avoid getting hurt or becoming ill. As the **environments** they are exploring are home to millions of other living things, they must also try to cause as little damage as possible. Some rainforest plants are very rare and must not be collected or damaged.

✂ SCIENCE SNAPSHOT

Searching for plants in the rainforest can be difficult sometimes simply because they are difficult to get to! Today, researchers in a part of French Guiana sail over the forest in airships to carry out research. Netting provides researchers with over 6,000 square feet of space to carry out their work and specimens are captured in special umbrellas.

For a long time many scientists regarded **rainforest** people's knowledge of the plants around them as worthless. Today, however, people are coming to realise that lots of the medicine they use is actually based on sound science. Many botanists start their search for medicinal plants by talking to people who live in the forest themselves, and reading the books they have written. This type of **botany** is called **ethnobotany**.

LISTENING TO LOCALS

Ethnobotanists study how people of a particular culture and region make of use of the plants around them. They believe that by going to the people who already use plants in the area that they can narrow down the search for useful medicinal plants. Ethnobotanists commission a doctor to come up with easy-to-understand descriptions and photographs of diseases. These descriptions are then given to **shamans** and other local healers. If a shaman or a healer recognises one of the diseases described, the plant treatment they recommend for that condition is written down by the ethnobotanist. If more than one shaman or healer describe a similar treatment for a disease, the plant is collected.

A shaman and his assistant scrape bark from a medicinal plant cut from a Peruvian rainforest.

A HEAD START?

One of the many advantages of speaking to locals is that they have been testing plants on people for thousands of years. They know which plants are poisonous, and can often spot subtle differences between similar looking plants that might not immediately be obvious to the botanist. In the rainforests of Samoa, for example, locals use the bark from a tree called Homalanthus nutans to treat hepatitis. However collecting the right kind of bark is not easy for an outsider. There is more than one variety of tree, and only one has the right kind of bark. Locals know that only trees of a certain size produce a useful extract, and harvesting bark from trees that are too small or too big is a waste of time.

SCIENCE CONCEPTS

ANIMALS AND MEDICINAL PLANTS

Ethnobotanists can learn from the animals in the rainforests, as well as the people who live there. Botanists in Brazil have noticed that wooly spider monkeys eat fruits of the "Monkey Ear" plant to increase their fertility. Laboratory tests have since shown that this plant does indeed promote fertility. Chimps have also been seen eating Aspilia and Vernonia (both Sunflower family) to treat infections and upset stomachs. Again, in the laboratory these plants have been shown to have an effect on stomach pains.

A Matses Indian shaman carries a bundle of medicinal plants gathered from rainforest near the Javari River, in the Amazon Basin, Peru.

FACT OR FICTION?

Ethnobotanists must also examine local myths, as there may be scientific truth behind them. For example, the ethno botanist Richard Gill was fascinated by a local legend that mongeese would eat the leaves of a plant called *Rauwolfia serpentia* to give it courage before fighting a cobra. Locals called the plant snakeroot and took it to treat a variety of mental disorders. When scientists **analysed** an extract of the plant, they found it was full of sedative chemicals and made an excellent treatment for high blood pressure.

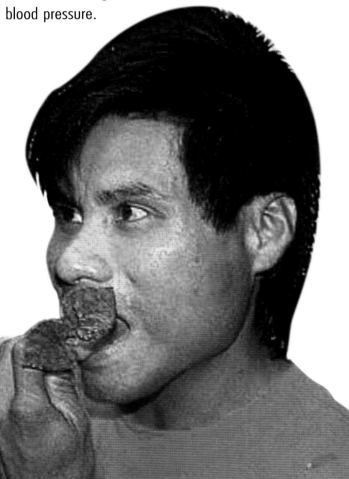

A Mayoruna Indian tastes the leaves of a medicinal plant while gathering natural remedies.

SCIENCE SNAPSHOT

For an ethnobotanist to become successful, they need to immerse themselves in the culture from which they are hoping to find plants from. A good ethnobotanist must usually know the language of the people they are studying, understand their culture and also gain their trust. To achieve these goals, ethnobotanists often stay in the **rainforests** for hundreds of hours at a time.

Once plants collected from the **rainforest** arrive at a major laboratory, scientists need to try and find out exactly what is inside them. A plant that has been used in traditional medicine for a specific purpose may contain one or more useful chemicals that can be extracted in the laboratory.

EXTRACTING AND TESTING

The first job of a research chemist presented with a potentially useful specimen is to extract the chemicals from the plant material. This can be done by grinding by hand in a pestle and mortar, or by using a special liquidiser. Adding water or another liquid will dissolve some of the chemicals that are in the plant material, and get rid of unwanted materials such as fats. Once the plant mixture is extracted, it is ready to be tested in the laboratory.

TESTING METHODS

Testing depends on what the research team are hoping to find. If a team wanted to develop a new **antibiotic**, for example, they would test a variety of plant extracts on **bacterial culture** dishes. A good antibiotic would inhibit or prevent the growth of bacterial colonies, but not harm the **cell** itself. In a poor antibiotic, the bacterial colonies would flourish and the cell may die. A plant that had a good effect on inhibiting bacteria at this stage would then enter the next testing stage, where chemists would begin to **analyse** the chemical structure of the extract.

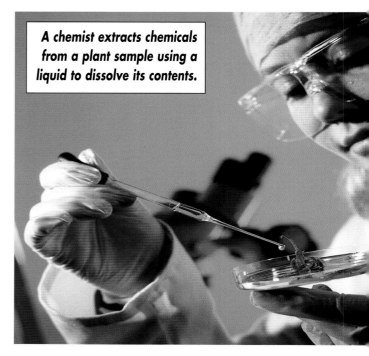

A chemist extracts chemicals from a plant sample using a liquid to dissolve its contents.

CHEMICAL SEARCH

If a plant extract has an effect in the screening tests, the next stage is to find out exactly what is inside the plant that is the active ingredient. To find out exactly how many different types of chemicals are in the mixture, chemists use a separation technique called thin layer **chromatography** (TLC). Tiny drops of the

SCIENCE CONCEPTS

TESTING WITH CELLS

Animal cells, including human cells, can be kept alive in the laboratory. They are kept in special dishes with a liquid that contains all the chemicals they need. These are put into **incubators** to keep the cells at body temperature. As the cells grow and divide, they are transferred to new dishes. Cells from one source are called a 'cell line'. Scientists know how each cell line normally grows, and so they can monitor the effects of adding the chemical that is being tested.

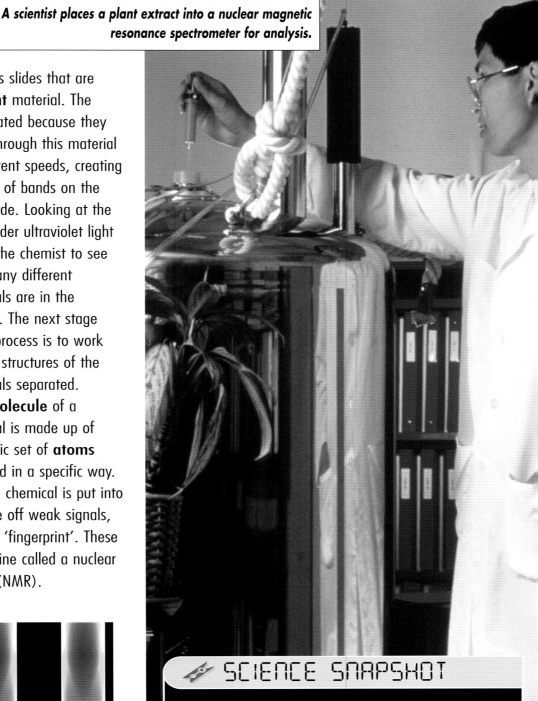

A scientist places a plant extract into a nuclear magnetic resonance spectrometer for analysis.

chemical mixture are put onto glass slides that are coated in a thin layer of **adsorbent** material. The chemicals in the mixture are separated because they

travel through this material at different speeds, creating a series of bands on the glass slide. Looking at the slide under ultraviolet light allows the chemist to see how many different chemicals are in the mixture. The next stage of the process is to work out the structures of the chemicals separated. Each **molecule** of a chemical is made up of a specific set of **atoms** arranged in a specific way. When a chemical is put into a magnetic field, its molecules give off weak signals, giving the chemical its own unique 'fingerprint'. These signals can be detected by a machine called a nuclear magnetic resonance spectrometer (NMR).

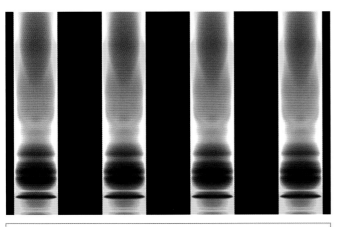

Coloured bands representing the separation of different chemicals by the process of chromatography.

SCIENCE SNAPSHOT

The Costa Rican firm INBio has signed an agreement with Merck **Pharmaceuticals**, the world's largest pharmaceutical firm, to provide Merck with plant and insect samples for research in return for money and laboratory equipment. If Merck successfully develops a **drug** from a sample provided by INBio, a portion of the money made will be used to support conservation programs in Costa Rica.

When scientists have extracted **chemicals** from plant material, they have to choose the ones that may have medicinal value. All medicines, including those from plants, can be put into groups depending on how they affect living **tissues**. The study of medicines and their actions is called **pharmacology** and scientists who do this work are called pharmacologists.

ALKALOIDS

Plants produce highly reactive chemicals known as **alkaloids**. Around 45% of tropical plants contain alkaloids, and these have a powerful effect on other living things. Those with similar structures often have similar effects on living tissues. Alkaloids can be grouped according to their **molecular** structures. The main groups are pyridines (e.g. nicotine), tropines (e.g. cocaine), quinolines (e.g. quinine), isoquinolines (e.g. morphine), phenethylamines (e.g. ephedrine) and indoles (e.g. tryptamine). Scientists already know the molecular structures of many alkaloids. Chemicals extracted from a plant sample that look similar to these are not really of interest. These are unlikely to be more successful in treating illness than existing **drugs**. Chemists are after unknown alkaloids that look very different to what they have seen before, and may prove to have medicinal value.

Poppy plants contain many alkaloids, some of which are used in medications including morphine and codeine.

SCIENCE CONCEPTS

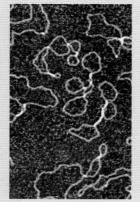

ANIMAL CELLS

Animals, including humans, are made up of millions of cells, which are organised into tissues and organs. Chemicals that act on individual cells or tissues just have a localised effect. Chemicals that act on whole organs or body systems will affect the whole body. Before scientists can decide whether a plant chemical can be turned into a useful drug, they need to test what it does to cells and tissues in the laboratory. For example, an extract that works on individual cells to stop them dividing might be a potential cure for cancer. The micrograph on the left shows how an anti-cancer drug binds to cancerous DNA, distorting its shape, killing the diseased affected cells.

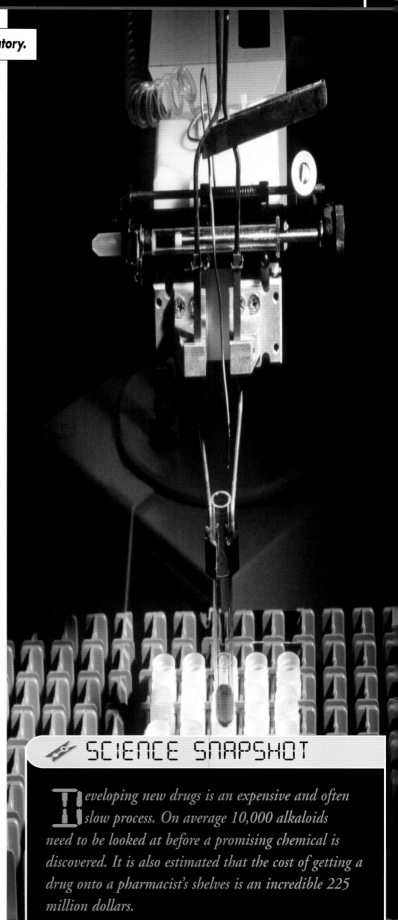

Robots can be used to test thousands of samples in the laboratory.

FINDING THE ONE

To find out whether alkaloids are likely to work or not, scientists take the individual chemicals from a plant into the testing process that was initially carried out on the entire plant extract. For example, each alkaloid from an extract shown to inhibit **bacteria** would be tested on **culture** dishes until the one responsible for inhibiting their growth was found. Researchers then know that this chemical has drug potential. Using robots can has revolutionized the amount of time it takes to test plant chemicals. On certain tests, thousands of samples can be examined in 24 hours. Sometimes, however it can still take many years to pinpoint the effective alkaloid. Researchers testing yew extract against cancerous cells were excited to see that it slowed down the **cancer**'s growth, but it took years of painstakingly eliminating all the many chemicals in the extract until the right one was located (*see pages 28-29*).

COPYING CHEMICALS

Once chemists know the structure of any chemical they are interested in, if they think it has the potential to be very useful, they may try to make it in the laboratory rather than harvesting thousands of plant specimens from the **rainforest**. They might take a similar chemical and try to modify it, or they may try to synthesize the new molecule completely from scratch. This is done by mixing some simple chemicals that will react together to make new substances. The new chemicals may be altered still further by adding other chemicals. This is does not always work, however. For example, while scientists are able to copy the cancer-fighting alkaloids from the Rosy periwinkle (*see page 24-25*), these do not work as well as chemicals taken from the original plant.

SCIENCE SNAPSHOT

Developing new drugs is an expensive and often slow process. On average 10,000 alkaloids need to be looked at before a promising chemical is discovered. It is also estimated that the cost of getting a drug onto a pharmacist's shelves is an incredible 225 million dollars.

All **drugs** have to undergo thorough testing in the laboratory before human trials begin. These tests are called toxicity tests. They are meant to minimize any unexpected side effects when they are eventually given to patients. If your doctor prescribes a medicine for you, he needs to be sure that it will be safe and will not harm you in any way.

TOXICOLOGISTS

Toxicologists

specialise in testing drugs to find out exactly how much of the medicine should be given and how often. They also test them to find out what sort of side effects there may be, and whether these change with bigger or smaller doses. They may test the drugs on **cell cultures** first and then test them on animals later. They may also test the drug in combination with other existing drugs to see if they interact in any way. Some interactions may be good — one or both drugs may work better in combination with the other. In other cases, however, one drug may alter the effect of the other, making it either dangerous or useless.

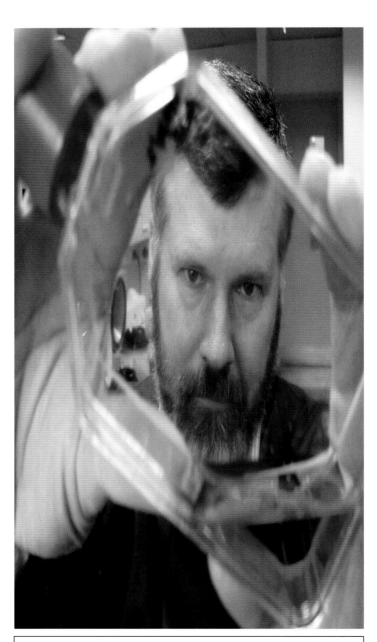

ABOVE: *A scientist examines a cell culture to see what effect a new antibiotic has had on it.* RIGHT: *A scanning electron micrograph image of human chromosomes.*

IN THE GENES

Our cells contain a substance called DNA (deoxyribonucleic acid). This is the **genetic** material that enables us to grow and function properly. In each cell, DNA is grouped into strands known as **chromosomes** - 46 in total. Scientists called geneticists investigate the safety of a new drug by looking at the effects of the medicine on the cell's **chromosomes**. They make sure the drug does not damage or change them in any way. Chromosome changes could lead to **cancer**. Also, if the drug affected the chromosomes in eggs and sperm, this might cause disease or deformity in any children that the patient might later have.

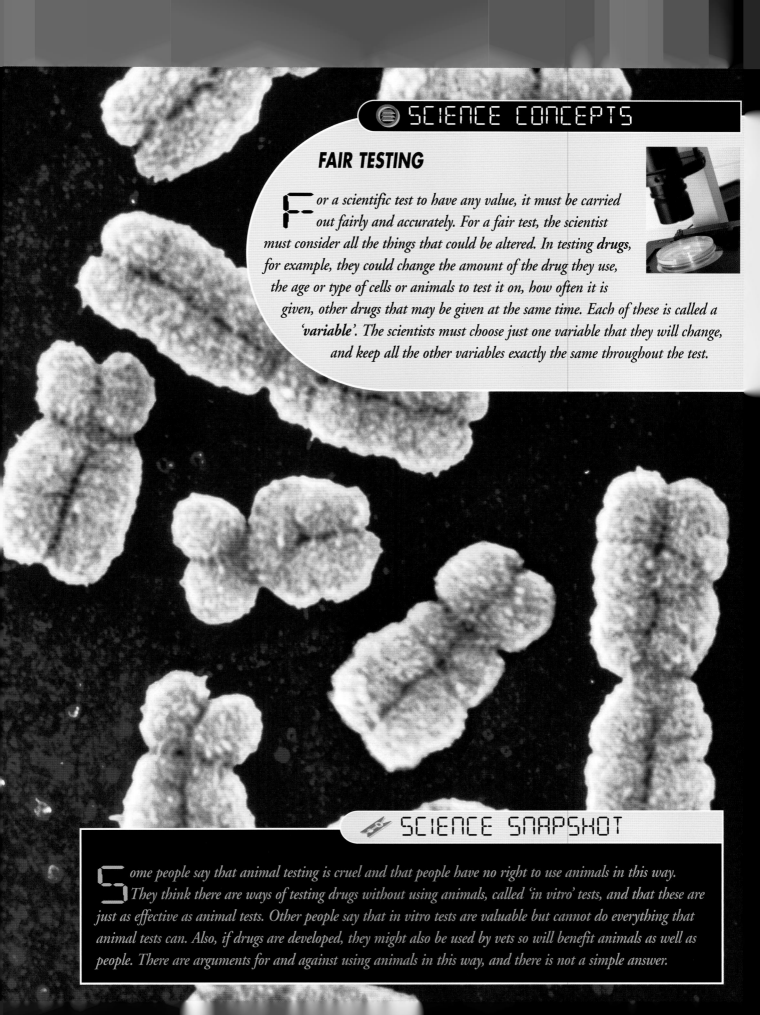

FAIR TESTING

For a scientific test to have any value, it must be carried out fairly and accurately. For a fair test, the scientist must consider all the things that could be altered. In testing **drugs**, for example, they could change the amount of the drug they use, the age or type of cells or animals to test it on, how often it is given, other drugs that may be given at the same time. Each of these is called a '**variable**'. The scientists must choose just one variable that they will change, and keep all the other variables exactly the same throughout the test.

Some people say that animal testing is cruel and that people have no right to use animals in this way. They think there are ways of testing drugs without using animals, called 'in vitro' tests, and that these are just as effective as animal tests. Other people say that in vitro tests are valuable but cannot do everything that animal tests can. Also, if drugs are developed, they might also be used by vets so will benefit animals as well as people. There are arguments for and against using animals in this way, and there is not a simple answer.

Even after toxicity tests have been carried out on a new **drug**, it needs to be tested on people before it can go onto the shelves of pharmacies. Doctors arrange a trial of the drug, and in most cases must make sure that their trial includes both men and women, as well as a full range of ages and ethnic origins.

A doctor holds up a new medication being tested as a possible treatment for depression.

TESTING IN HUMANS

Testing a new drug in humans is called a 'clinical trial' and usually follows four stages. The first stage involves giving the drug to a small number of healthy volunteers or patients. Doctors look to see what if any side effects are caused by the drug, and observe what doses can be taken safely. If there are no serious side effects, stage two of the test begins. This involves giving the drug to people who have the illness researchers hope the drug will be able to treat. If the drug has had a positive effect stage three begins, which involves giving the drug to a much larger group of people, sometimes as many as several thousand. This stage can take several years before results can be known. The final stage is conducted after a drug is approved, and takes the form of ongoing studies in large numbers of patients who have been prescribed the drug by their doctors. If any side-effects are found, they must be mentioned in the packaging by the drug manufacturer.

SCIENCE CONCEPTS

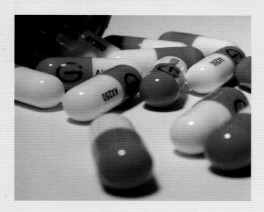

TRICKING THE MIND

Some doctors think that if your brain thinks you are taking medicine even when you are not, you have a more positive state of mind and this might have a healing effect. Since the 1950s, many studies have shown that taking a placebo treatment can be almost as effective as taking genuine medicine. Consistently, the patients who have responded best in trials have been the ones who have the greatest belief in the treatment they are taking and the most positive mental outlook.

A male nurse gives some medication to a patient in a hospital ward.

MAKING IT FAIR

To be sure that a drug trial is fair, one group of patients may be given a normal treatment; another the new treatment that is being tested, and a third group may be given a **placebo** (see Science Concepts). The doctors then know that any difference in results really is due to the drugs themselves and not just a altered stage of mind. Sometimes, an even stricter system known as 'double blind' is used. This means that neither the doctors nor the patients know which treatment they are receiving. Only when all the data has been collected is it revealed exactly to whom the medicine was given.

MEASURING THE EFFECT

Scientists need to decide in advance about how they will measure the drug's effect. In some cases, they can have a definite measure. For example, cholesterol levels in the blood can be measured accurately by a simple blood test. By doing this both before and after the new drug is given, doctors can find out exactly how effective the drug has been. In other cases, the patients themselves may have to answer detailed questions about how they feel. For example, if a drug is designed to work as a painkiller, a patient may be asked to make a note of their pain levels at regular intervals. These notes will give doctors an indication of how effective the drug is and how long its effects last.

Blood tests can sometimes give a clear result as to whether a medicine has worked or not.

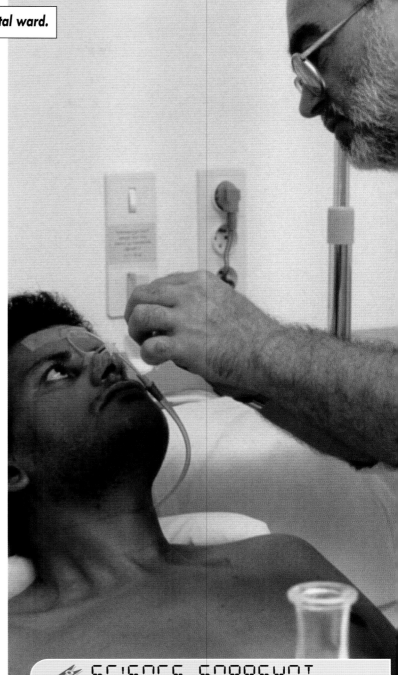

SCIENCE SNAPSHOT

In a trial where a potentially life and death situation is being looked at, results have to be constantly monitored. In tests of the AIDS drug zidovudine (AZT), patients receiving the drug were having a markedly better effect than those receiving the placebo. Scientists immediately called an end to the trial, and every patient on the test was given the drug before it was approved for general use.

Scientists are constantly searching for chemicals that will cure a wide variety of diseases including **cancer**, **AIDS** and many others. There are millions of plants that may yield potentially useful chemicals – nobody knows when or where the next fantastic discovery may be made!

STOPPING THE DESTRUCTION

We are in danger of completely destroying the **rainforests** and everything that lives in them. Once they covered 15% of the Earth's surface - now the figure is 7%. However, many organizations are trying to put a stop to this destruction.

Organizations such as the Rainforest Foundation, for example, have helped by purchasing over eight million acres of rainforest and handing it to local people whom have been trained in sensitive farming and harvesting methods. People are also becoming more aware of the need to use **sustainable** wood. A good example of this is the fact that the Olympic torches for the 2004 Games were all made from wood approved by the Rainforest Alliance.

More than 30 millions acres of rainforest are destroyed every year. If logging continues at the current rate, the rainforest will completely disappear within the next 40 years.

WORKING WITH LOCALS

Drug companies need to search these **habitats** for potentially important sources of medicines. Many are now taking great care to work with local communities, and are trying to collect and record their traditional uses of plants. These records could form the basis of future scientific investigations.

Databases are being set up to make this information available to scientists all over the world. For example, The People and Plants Initiative, a partnership between **WWF**, **UNESCO** and The Royal Botanic Gardens, Kew, is carrying out work like this. It means that people will be able to access information without having to collect and test the plant again. It will offer some protection to rare plants and precious habitats.

SCIENCE CONCEPTS

RAINFOREST INSECTS AND ANIMALS

Scientists are not just looking at plants in the rainforest, but also the many animals and insects that depend on these plants. Insects in particular are being screened for **phytochemicals** - plant-based drugs. Drugs that stop blood from clotting have been found in blood-sucking rainforest insects such as mosquitos, for example. A new painkilling drug is also being developed from the poison of a rainforest-dwelling tree frog (left), which makes users alert rather than sleepy like most other painkillers.

By working with locals like this Cofan Indian from the Ecuadorian rainforest, drugs companies are learning more about the plants there and what benefits they might offer.

A FAIR DEAL?

In the past, many plants were taken from the rainforests and used by large companies to make drugs. The companies made a lot of money from this, but gave very little back to the areas from where the plants were taken. Efforts are being made to stop this happening and many companies now try to ensure that local communities also benefit and receive some share of the profits made from the discoveries. An example of such co-operation is between, the drug company Hoffmann LaRoche and Costa Rica. The drug company funded a full survey of the wildlife in Costa Rica in exchange for plant specimens. The drug company also agreed to share the profits of any drug made from Costa Rican plants with the Costa Rican government.

SCIENCE SNAPSHOT

Tourism is being used in many countries to protect the rainforest. In Peru, for example, the Amazon Centre for Environmental Education (ACEER) receives its funding from several travel companies. These businesses take individuals into the rainforests to experience the unique life within them, and also pledge to donate a share of the profits towards conservation.

Rosy periwinkle is a small, evergreen plant with pale pink and purple flowers. Its botanical name is Catharanthus roseus, and it is also known as Madagascar periwinkle because it is one of the island's native plants. There are other types of periwinkle too, and traditionally these plants have been used to treat many different conditions, including **diabetes**, wasp stings, and coughs.

Two African girls clutch a sprig of the Rosy periwinkle, a traditional cure for many diseases.

Despite extensive deforestation, the island of Madagascar still has over 10,000 km of rainforest left.

MADAGASCAN MIRACLE

Western researchers first became interested in the Madagascar periwinkle in the 1950's. These scientists were trying to find a treatment for **diabetes**, and they heard that, during the Second World War, some American soldiers had used Madagascar periwinkle leaves when they could not get any insulin. They also heard that some people in Jamaica used a tea from the leaves as a diabetes treatment. Two separate groups of researchers began investigating the plant — Beer and Noble in Canada and Svoboda in America. They found that the plant leaves contained more than seventy **alkaloids**. Beer and Noble extracted and purified one that they called vinblastine. Svoboda isolated another that they called vincristine. The 'vin' part of the names comes from 'Vinca' which is the old botanical name for periwinkle.

AN UNEXPECTED FINDING

The scientists found that neither of the chemicals had much effect on blood sugar levels, so they were not going to be effective as treatments for diabetes. However, the scientists injected an extract of whole periwinkle plant into mice that had **leukaemia** – and found that the mice lived longer than they would normally have done. The first human tests were carried out in 1960.

A 49-year old man who was dying from leukaemia was treated with vinblastine, with spectacular results. Within one week he was able to walk again and four months later he was cured. Now vincristine is the main **drug** used to treat leukaemia in children and vinblastine is used to treat **Hodgkin's disease** in adults. The discovery and development of these two drugs has saved a very large number of lives.

BETTER THAN THE ORIGINAL?

Both vincristine and vinblastine work in a similar way. In leukaemia, white blood **cells** get out of control and divide over and over again, making the patient very ill. Vincristine and vinblastine work by inhibiting the process of cell division. Although these drugs can now be made in the laboratory, scientists have found that the **synthetic** chemicals are not as effective as the ones extracted from the periwinkle plants.

CASE STUDY FACTFILE

- *The whole plant is used to make the drugs vincristine and vinblastine.*
- *These medications fight cancer by stopping white blood cells dividing.*
- *Annual sales of vincristine and vinblastine are over $100 million.*
- *None of this money goes back to help the people of the impoverished country of Madagascar.*

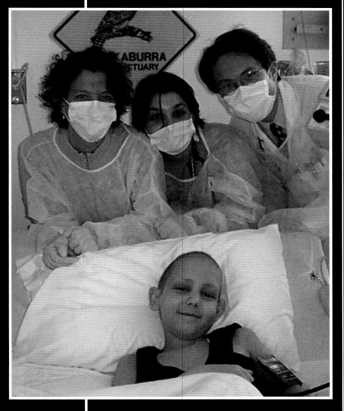

Vincristine extracted from the Rosy periwinkle can stop leukaemia by preventing cells multiplying.

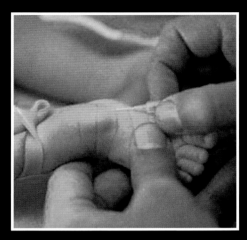

A baby with muscle spasms is given curare.

Curare comes from a vine called Chondrodendro tomentosum that is native to the Amazon rainforest. The vine climbs as high as thirty metres into the rainforest canopy. Curare was traditionally used by Amazonian Indians as a poison spread on the points of arrows and blowdarts. Today, however, scientists are finding out that, used correctly, the plant may have many beneficial effects on our health.

HANDLE WITH CARE!

Although curare can be deadly, curare does not act in the same way as other poisons. Its active chemical, turbocurarine, stops signals from the brain reaching the muscles. This makes the muscles relax, paralysing the victim. When the muscles of the chest and abdomen relax, breathing stops and the victim dies of **asphyxiation**. Curare is not **absorbed** by the digestive system, so it is safe to eat meat from animals killed in this way.

READY TO RELAX

Curare has also been used in South America as a traditional **herbal remedy**. The roots are used as a **diuretic** and fever reducer and are also rubbed onto bruises. The crushed leaves are used to treat snake bites. Curare was first reported in Europe in the 16th century by Sir Walter Raleigh, an English Elizabethan sailor and explorer. In 1912, a German surgeon called Arthur Lawen first reported that it could be used to relax a patient's

muscles during surgery. Two Canadian doctors, Griffith and Johnson, investigated this and their trials in 1942 showed that this was true. It is now routinely used in some surgery where it is important for muscles to remain relaxed, although the patient's breathing has to be supported mechanically. Curare can also be used in the treatment of **tetanus**. Because curare relaxes muscles, it prevents the muscle spasm and paralysis caused by tetanus **bacteria**.

FRANKLYN'S CIGARETTES.

QUEEN ELIZABETH & SIR W. RALEIGH

MORE SECRETS?

In addition to tubocurarine, curare contains a lot of other chemicals. These have not yet been fully investigated, but it is likely that scientists will discover many other medicinal uses of this plant. Current research shows that it may have a ro in reducing nausea and vomiting, and as an anti-anxiety treatment.

Famous for introducing tobacco to Europe, Sir Walter Raleigh also brought back Curare from the Americas.

The Jagua people of South America still use darts tipped with curare to hunt with. In the West, people are now discovering the more positive uses of the plant.

CASE STUDY FACTFILE

- *Curare was used by Amazonian Indians as a poison for arrow tips. Its name comes from two Tupi Indian words meaning 'bird' and 'to kill'.*
- *The vine is only poisonous if it gets into the bloodstream - it can be eaten quite safely.*
- *The vine from which Curare comes also produces a fruit which can be eaten quite safely.*
- *Curare is used in some countries as an anaesthetic.*
- *It may have other medicinal uses that have not yet been studied.*

The vine Chondrodendrom tomtomentosum is often called velvet leaf because the underside of its heart-shaped leaves are covered in tiny soft hairs.

The eucalyptus tree, Eucalyptus globulus, is a tall, evergreen tree with long, blue-green leaves. It is native to Australia and Tasmania, and is the only food that koala bears eat! The leaves contain a fresh-smelling oil that was used as a **remedy** by Australian Aborigines for a wide variety of illnesses including fever, wounds, coughs and joint pain. The oil that is extracted from the leaves is known as eucalyptol.

The German botanist Baron Ferdinand von Muller.

IT CAME FROM GERMANY

A German botanist, Baron Ferdinand von Muller, introduced eucalyptus to the west in the mid 19th century. He thought it would be an excellent disinfectant, and it was used as such for many years. It has also been found to be useful in industry, and in making perfumes. Eucalyptol has been found to work in two main ways. It contains chemicals called tannins which, when **inhaled,** can reduce inflammation of the linings of the nose and airways. This is why it is found as an ingredient in many cough sweets and other remedies for colds. Its other main use is in creams rubbed onto the skin. As it is **absorbed** into the skin, it stimulates blood flow, which helps to relieve pain in muscles and joints.

A NEW USE

Wounds on an Australian pig called Beau Rowan were cured by the use of a eucalyptus dressing.

A potential new use for the oil was uncovered on the outskirts of Sydney with a pig called Beau Rowan. Beau Rowan had an infected wound on his back leg that would not heal, and his owner thought he would have to be killed. As a last resort, a eucalyptus dressing was put on the wound — within three weeks the infection had vanished and the wound was completely healed! Scientists at the University of Sydney have since tried using eucalyptus oil, mixed with other plant oils (including lemon, thyme and cloves), to treat infections in hospital patients in whom other **antibiotics** have failed. They have found the mixture to be amazingly effective, with more than two thirds of the patients completely cured. The mixture is still being tested and is not widely available as a treatment yet, but scientists are hopeful that eucalyptus might prove to be a cure for hospital 'superbugs'.

Eucalyptus is probably best known as the favourite food of the Australian Koala bear.

- *Eucalyptus was traditionally used by Australian Aborigines to treat a variety of conditions.*
- *It became known in Western countries in the 19th century and was used as a disinfectant.*
- *Many remedies for coughs and colds contain eucalyptus oil.*
- *Current research suggests it may be a very powerful antibiotic.*

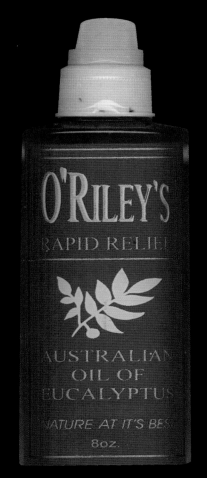

Sprays and ointments containing Eucalyptus Oil which can be used to treat minor injuries are now on sale.

Taxos brevifola is a small evergrown tree that grows in parts of the United States. It is also known as the Pacific Yew and is a very slow growing plant. Much of the tree's **habitat** has been cleared for growing trees for timber. However, in the 1960s, rumours started to circulate that the bark of the Pacific Yew had **cancer**-fighting properties.

A GREAT DISCOVERY

The distinctive reddish bark of the Pacific Yew.

In 1962, botanists collected a bag of yew bark and sent it to the laboratories of the National Cancer Institute. When scientists extracted material from the bark and looked at it under a microscope, they discovered that the extract was packed with mysterious **alkaloids**. Tested against cancerous **cells**, the Pacific extract seemed to slow down the growth of the cancer. Excited by this possibility, the extract was injected into mice with leukemia, and again seemed to have positive results. In 1967, the chemical that was working against the cancer was isolated, and given the name taxol. However, at the time the National Cancer Institute were investigating several other plant extracts, and nothing further was done with taxol. It was not until the late 1970s that more work was carried out to discover how taxol worked. Scientists testing tiny samples of taxol against various cancers were amazed to discover that taxol had totally stopped the cells dividing. In 1982, the first human trials of Taxol began. Because Taxol could not be dissolved in water,

it was mixed with a substance called cremophore. Unfortunately, this mix proved disasterous, and a couple of patients died as a result of receiving treatment. In 1985, larger trials began and taxol's effect on women with ovarian cancer were stunning. By 1989, taxol was being tried on other form of cancers, including head, breast and lung cancer. Everybody was enthusiastic about the **drug**, but there was one big problem. There were not enough Pacific Yew trees available to treat everyone who might benefit from taxol.

HUMAN TESTS

Conservationists were worried that the Pacific Yew might be driven into extinction if it continued to be harvested at the current rate. However, chemists had no luck trying to **synthesise** the drug in the laboratory. It was not until 1993 that taxol was finally successfully copied by scientists. A chemist called Robert Holton found a way to reproduce the chemical from a common form of yew. Drugs companies could

A researcher checks Pacific Yew plants being dried, before the extraction of the drug taxol.

CASE STUDY
FACTFILE

- *Making taxol from the Pacific Yew requires a lot of trees. It takes an average of six to treat each patient.*
- *In the past, yew has been used to poison rather than heal people!*
- *Taxol has been hailed as the most important cancer drug of the last 15 years by scientists.*
- *Taxol not only stops cancer cells dividing, but it makes it hard for them to ever start growing again.*

now get as much taxol as they wanted from common yew trees. In the future, it might also be possible to make taxol from a fungus that grows on yew bark, growing these fungi in the laboratory. Two drugs from the yew tree, Taxol (paclitaxel) and Taxotere (docetaxel) are currently considered to be the most important drugs in cancer chemotherapy.

INTO THE FUTURE

Today, some scientists think that taxol can be made even more effective if it is taken in combination with other drugs. Researchers in America believe that a chemical from the rainforest Lapacho tree (beta-lapachone) can strengthen the effect of taxol if it is administered before the drug. Tests on mice wiped out tumors and didn't cause any significant side effects. Clinical trials are planned in the near future and it is hoped that the combination will be used in the future to treat stubborn cancers such as prostate cancer.

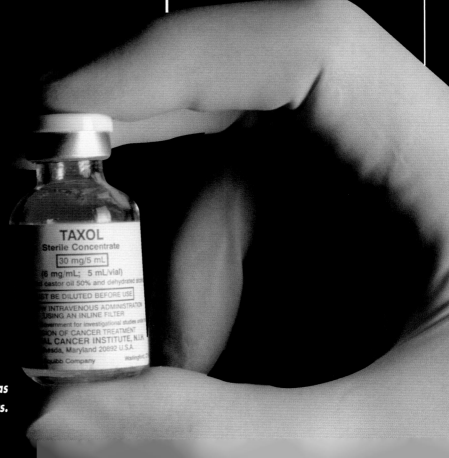

A pharmacist holds a bottle of Taxol, a drug which has proved highly effective against certain types of tumours.

absorb to soak up

adsorbent a material that allows another substance to pass into it

AIDS an illness that severely weakens the body's ability to protect itself from viruses, infections and some cancers

alkaloid a chemical, usually from a plant, that has a chemical effect on other living things

analyse to find out all the parts of something

antibiotic a chemical that destroys bacteria and other micro-organisms

asthma chronic respiratory disease that causes the sufferer to have difficulty breathing during an attack

asphyxiation to prevent something receiving any oxygen

atom the smallest unit of an element

bacteria a type of micro-organism

biochemistry the study of the chemistry of living things

botany the study of plants

cancer an illness in which cells divide uncontrollably

cell one of the millions of tiny units from which all living things are made

chemistry the study of materials and what they are made of

chromosome strand of genetic material

chromatography separation of chemicals across an adsorbent surface

Conservation the protection, preservation, management, or restoration of wildlife and of natural resources

control an untreated group in a test, used for comparison with treated groups

culture to grow artificially in the laboratory

database a system for organising and storing information on a computer

diabetes – the popular name for diabetes mellitus, a disease that affects the body's ability to process sugar.

deforestation the removal of trees

distillation separation of dissolved substances from liquids by evaporating and condensing

diuretic a drug that increases water loss from the body

drug a chemical that has a pharmacological effect

environment the world around us

ethnobotany the study of how people use plants within their local environment

genetics the study of heredity

habitat the place where a plant or animal lives

herbal to do with plants

heredity the passing of

characteristics from one generation to the next

Hodgkin's disease disease in which the lymph nodes, spleen and liver are enlarged

incubator a machine that maintains a constant temperature

inhale to breathe in

leukaemia a type of cancer in which the production of normal blood cells is suppressed

malaria a disease carried by mosquitoes, common in tropical places

molecule the smallest unit of a substance that can exist on its own

organism - Single life form, such as an animal, fungus, plant or bacterium

pharmaceutical to do with medicines

pharmacology the study of the effect of chemicals on living tissues

phytochemical a chemical found in plants

phytochemistry the study of chemicals in plants

placebo an inactive treatment used as a control in drug trials

rainforest forests that grow in warm, wet areas of the world

remedy treatment for illness or disease

sampling collecting objects such as plants for examination

shaman - Somebody who acts as a medium between the spirit world and the visible world, and who uses magic as a way of healing people

species a type of animal or plant

spectrometer an instrument used in the analysis of chemicals

superbug - Type of bacteria that is resistant to antibiotics

sustainable - Capable of being sustained. For example, a way of cutting down trees in a rainforest without destroying the habitat

synthetic - Something man-made, not of natural origin

tetanus - disease where various muscles spontaneously contract

tissue - part of the body's building blocks. There are four types of tissue: There are four basic types of tissue: muscle, nerve, epidermal, and connective.

toxicology the study of poisons and their actions on living tissues

tropical something found in the tropics, a region of the earth's surface characterised by hot and wet climate

vaccination treatment to provide immunity to a specific disease

variable a factor that must be controlled in scientific tests

vulnerable species whose status is threatened by declining numbers

Copyright © ticktock Entertainment Ltd 2004
First published in Great Britain in 2004 by ticktock Media Ltd.,
Unit 2, Orchard Business Centre, North Farm Road, Tunbridge Wells, Kent, TN2 3XF
We would like to thank: Elizabeth Wiggans and Jenni Rainford for their help with this book.
ISBN 1 86007 593 2 HB   ISBN 1 86007 587 8 PB
Printed in China
A CIP catalogue record for this book is available from the British Library.

All rights reserved. No part of this publication may be reproduced, copied, stored in a retrieval system, or transmitted in any form or by any means electronic, mechanical, photocopying, recording or otherwise without prior written permission of the copyright owner.

Picture Credits
Alamy: 4-5c, 5t, 7r, 9t, 14c, 18cl, 18bl, 19 all, 20 all,. Art Archive: 24cb, 26tl. Corbis: 10bl, 11 all, 22cl, 22-23 c, 23br, 24tl, 26c.
Bodleian Library: 6cl. Science Photo Library: 2-3, 5r, 5-6c, 8cl, 8bl, 10c, 12b, 13 all, 14b, 15r, 16c, 17 all, 24c, 25r, 27c, 28-29 all.